A Pastor/Leader's Guide for

Bridges of Promise

JUDSON
CHURCH MEMBERSHIP RESOURCES
For Growing Disciples

OLDER
CHILDREN

A Pastor/Leader's Guide for

Bridges of Promise

Taking Steps to Follow Jesus

Virginia A. Sargent, Editor

Page design: Judith I. Gotwald
Cover design: Jim Gerhard

BRIDGES OF PROMISE: TAKING STEPS TO FOLLOW JESUS
PASTOR/LEADER'S GUIDE

Contents:

Dr. Paul Nichols
1939-1990

As we neared completion of the Church Membership/ Discipleship project, we were shocked and saddened by the death of one who shared with us in the creation of and expectations for these new resources.

Dr. Paul Nichols was a friend and colleague. He was the source of inspiration in the early phases of the project. As a person who was above all else a pastor, he understood the need for resources that would enable persons to become followers of Jesus Christ.

This discipleship series is offered as an expression of thanksgiving for Paul's life and as a challenge for others to maintain the concern for the nurturing of all persons in the Christian life, a concern that was paramount in the ministry of Paul Nichols.

Foreword

At last! New Baptist church membership training materials! Because these have long been asked for by pastors and Christian education leaders of American Baptist Churches, the Board of Educational Ministries has now developed an excellent set of resources that serve well to prepare persons for church membership as well as a whole life of following Jesus Christ as Sovereign and Savior.

Since Baptists emphasize the local churches as building blocks of the Kingdom, the need for participation in the local church is foundational to these resources. Throughout all the resources the individualism that results from much evangelism is balanced by the realization that a Christian life and mission is no solo flight. Christians simply must live and function in community.

Central to these resources is the understanding that persons must make faith their own, whatever the route or process by which they come to trust in Jesus. Recognizing valid biblical norms for faith and living out that faith, the resources do not stereotype either conversion or the life of discipleship.

I am pleased that from the beginning the design of these resources has included children, youth, and adult materials and that the first two were not mere afterthoughts. The resources take seriously the gospel tradition and faith development, clearly recognizing that children, youth, and adults come to faith in different ways. On this point they are consonant with our approach to evangelism that meets people where they are—culturally, in terms of age, spiritual understanding, and so forth.

A *systemic evangelism* is taken seriously, encouraging that evangelism be built into the whole fabric of the church's educational program.

"Costly discipleship"—the call to a commitment to serve Christ in the church and the world—is part of the scope of the resources.

That all of the membership/discipleship resources were prepared by "practitioners" is ultimately the strength of the enterprise. And, that the material was developed by women and men, by people of all races, attests to the fact that our churches are no longer monochromatic. The resources were prepared for the world of today and the marvelously inclusive church God has called forth for these times.

Emmett V. Johnson
Director of Evangelism
American Baptist Churches in the U.S.A.

Preface

From earliest times Baptists have emphasized the *quality* of the church's life. They have insisted on the necessity of Christian experience as the basis for church membership. The church is a fellowship of *believers*, we have said, and entry into the church should be preceded by evidence of faith in Jesus Christ and a life-changing personal relationship to God in the Holy Spirit. A regenerate church should lead to "visible saints," Christians who not only speak of their Christian experience, but who live it out in deed. Because such a view of church membership required scrutiny of a person's testimony and practice, infant membership was rejected as unscriptural. The "believer's church" remains still a foundational concept in Baptist identity.

It follows that the regenerate church is a "gathered" body, not a geographical parish. This, too, has consistently distinguished Baptists from many other communions. What matters is not the boundaries of a neighborhood, but the reality of our relationship to Christ and the character of our experience of the gospel.

American Baptists: A Unifying Vision, p. 29

Because we Baptists are the type of church we are, we bear an exceptional responsibility for the introduction and orientation of persons to the community of faith.

Such responsibility cannot be left to happenstance. The Judson Church Membership Resources are intended to support you in the life-shaping, church-shaping, task of welcoming new members.

New members come from at least two sources. There are those who come as a result of lifetime nurturing by family and church. For them membership is, perhaps, a natural step. They possess a basic biblical understanding and a personal awareness of the meaning of church membership. The special type of preparation caught up by church membership classes is for these persons a time for pulling together and seeing in one context the meaning of the step they are taking.

Other persons come to membership out of comparatively, or totally, non-church backgrounds. Their introduction to Jesus Christ and the community of faith may have been one of great emotion. Their eagerness should not detract from the need to help them examine, too, the step they are taking.

Membership preparation—orientation, and both initial and ongoing support of new Christians—is an essential responsibility for a church that proclaims a regenerate church membership.

The purpose of the Judson church membership/discipleship materials, is to support you in the accomplishment of that responsibility.

It is probable that in the majority of American Baptist churches, pastors, associate pastors and ministers of Christian education carry the responsibility for membership preparation. Because of that fact, these resources have been prepared especially for *you*. It is appropriate to point out that the Judson Church Membership Resources have been prepared *by* practitioners *for* practitioners.

In January of 1988 a group of such persons, representing the diversity of American Baptist churches, supported by staff members of the Board of Educational Ministries, met to plan a new set of church membership resources for American Baptists. The group included:*

- Dr. Paul Nichols, Chair, Pastor
  Good Shepherd Baptist Church, Richmond, Virginia
- Rev. Tom Bayes, Pastor
  Judson Memorial Baptist Church, Lansing, Michigan
- Rev. Doug Beyer, Pastor
  First Baptist Church, Temple City, California
- Rev. James Braker, Pastor
  Emmanuel Baptist Church, Ridgewood, New Jersey
- Rev. Wendell Brooker, Pastor
  Fairview Community Church (American Baptist), Cleveland, Ohio
- Rev. Sara Day Cheesman, Associate Pastor
  South Wayne Baptist Church, Fort Wayne, Indiana
- Rev. Frank Clayton, Staff
  American Baptist Churches of Maine, Augusta, Maine
- Rev. Paulita García, Associate Executive Minister
  Baptist Churches of Puerto Rico, Hato Rey, Puerto Rico

*The titles listed refer to positions held at the time of the meeting.

- Rev. Linda Hart, Pastor
  North Hunterdon Baptist Church, Glen Gardner, New Jersey
- Rev. Rose Johnson, Co-pastor
  First Baptist Church of Oregon City, Oregon City, Oregon
- Rev. Gloria Kesselring, Director of Christian Education
  Emmanuel Baptist Church, Parkersburg, West Virginia
- Rev. Sylvia Kinard, Associate Pastor
  Brown Memorial Baptist Church, Brooklyn, New York
- Rev. Frank Nelson, Pastor
  Woodbury Baptist Church, Woodbury, Minnesota
- Rev. Noah Osborne, Minister of Christian Education
  McGee Avenue Baptist Church, Berkeley, California
- Rev. Mark Wilson, Associate Pastor
  Hartford Avenue Baptist Church, Detroit, Michigan

Educational Ministries Staff persons involved were:

- Rev. John "Bud" Carroll, Director
  Division of Church Education
- Rev. Joe Leonard, Director
  Department of Adult Ministries and Administration
  Division of Church Education
- Rev. Don Ng, Director
  Department of Ministry with Youth
  Division of Church Education
- Ms. Kristy Arnesen Pullen, Senior Editor
  Division of Publishing
- Ms. Esther Pullis, Director
  Department of Ministry with Children
  Division of Church Education
- Rev. Bud Wilmot, Program Associate
  Department of Ministry with Children
  Division of Church Education

During the period of development, the planners and writers were supported by the "Committee of 100." This group, comprising men and women in pastoral leadership positions representing all types of churches, geographical distribution, theological opinions, and racial background, reviewed manuscripts and provided answers to questions essential to the development of resources.

The value of the services of all these practitioners—the Planning Team and Committee of 100—cannot be too greatly affirmed. Because of their work our goal, resources by and for practitioners, has been achieved.

The Judson Church Membership Resources include a new member/disciple book and pastor/leader's guide for three age levels—children, youth, and adult.

Bridges of Promise, the children's material written by Franklin W. Nelson, introduces children in grades five and six to a life of faith by explaining God's promises to us and Jesus' role as the bridge leading us to God. The pastor/leader's guide includes session-by-session suggestions for using the material, as well as additional articles on children's faith development and on what can be done for children seeking baptism who may be too young to understand its meaning.

Storyweaving: You and Your Faith Journey, the youth material written by Wendell Brooker, includes *A Disciple's Guidebook*, a *Pastor/Leader's Guide*, and a *Mentor's Guide* to help youth weave their own stories into the Christian story and the story of Baptist tradition. Guided by the pastor or leader and a personal mentor, youth can weave the threads of their lives into rewarding new lives as disciples of Jesus Christ and members of their local Baptist churches.

The Family of God, by Douglas Beyer, is a handbook for adult disciples of Jesus Christ, explaining both the privileges and the responsibilities involved in being a member of God's family. The accompanying pastor/leader's guide offers suggestions for using *The Family of God* in a classroom setting and includes sections on faith development and the biblical foundation for discipleship.

We hope this collection of resources assists you as a church leader in welcoming and enabling the new disciples in your midst.

John "Bud" Carroll

Discipleship Course for Children

A Prologue

From Gretchen Kleinsasser, a former Christian education director and a mother who used this material with her son Zach

Bridges of Promise as a title for this discipleship program formed a valuable word picture for me. As the adult leader, I could see a starting point, a direction to follow, and a goal to reach.

I had the opportunity to go through this course with my son. It was of great value for us to work through this material together as parent and child. I was able to see my son in a different light. As we read and talked and even argued through the study, I learned who my son was and how his mind worked. I had never taken the time or even thought it very important to meet him on this very different level. I found a depth to my son's intellect and emotions that I had not been aware of before. He showed me a sensitivity and willingness that was not a normal part of his everyday persona.

It was exciting for me to lead my son through the decision-making process of accepting Christ as Lord and Savior. Just as it was a commitment for my son, it became a renewed commitment for myself. Zach was beginning to understand, and I was expanding my understanding. He was developing discipline, and I was challenged to remain disciplined as well.

I appreciate very much the input of our pastor, Frank Nelson, throughout this discipleship process. The warmth and caring that Frank has shown us is the same warmth and caring that is reflected so well in the discipleship materials he has written.

Gretchen Kleinsasser

Introductory Notes

To: Spiritual Guides of Children
From: The Writer

Dear Pastor, Parent, Grandparent, or Adult Friend of a Child,

What does it mean to be a spiritual guide?

John Westerhoff has said, "Our question ought never to be, how can we make our children into Christians? Rather it must be, how can we be Christian with our children?" (*Bringing Up Children in the Christian Faith*, Minneapolis: Winston Press, 1980, p. 29).

As you relate in a special way with one or more children during the coming weeks, the question that needs to be asked is less, How can I make this child into a Christian, but more, How can I be a person of God with this child? Can I live and love and demonstrate the grace of God in such a way that it is good news?

Someone once said that faith in God is something that is caught, not taught. But how is it caught? Perhaps it is through the quality of our relationship with the child.

God initiates the relationship and comes to us in person—Jesus Christ. God continues the relationship and comes to us through people, the church. As a spiritual guide to one child or several children, you are the representative of Christ and the church with those children. The Holy Spirit is at work in your life and the children's lives to allow you all to experience spiritual growth through this study. Through your relationship, faith can be caught.

—Prepare for this relationship through prayer. Spend large blocks of time in prayer. Pray specifically and daily for the child or children who are under your guidance. Invite others you know to pray for the child or children as well.

—Prepare for this relationship by getting acquainted with the child or children and with the families, if possible.

—Prepare for this relationship through study. Study the materials carefully and work through the daily activities so that you will be at least one week ahead of the children. The materials work well with children in the fifth and sixth grades.

—Prepare for this relationship through planning. Plan ahead of time to make this an affirming experience for the child or children. Send cards, make or purchase gifts. You may even want to plan to do something just for fun, such as an outdoor activity, a movie, or a shared meal.

Realize that not all children who participate in this study will make a decision to follow Christ as Lord and Savior and be baptized. The role of the spiritual guide is not to make that happen or to force the decision. Honor the child or children with your love, acceptance, and faith. Allow the Holy Spirit of God to work through your relationship. The miracle of monarch wings may become the promise fulfilled in God's time.

To: Pastors
From: The Writer

Dear Pastor,

The traditional "Pastor's Class" has been one of the most prominent ways in which evangelism takes place in the church. The materials presented to you are for use in pastor's classes with children. As pastor, you are a key person in making decisions about the form the classes may take. The material has been written with flexibility as a prominent feature. Following are several models you may want to consider:

—a pastor meeting with two or more children for eight weekly or biweekly sessions lasting one to two hours;

—a pastor one-on-one with a child;

—a pastor guiding a child and another adult (such as a parent, grandparent, church school teacher, adult friend); in which case, Chapters 1 and 6 especially would need to be done with the help of the pastor.

—a pastor guiding a group of two or more children with their spiritual guides (parent, grandparent, or other adult friend of each child). The pastor would meet with the adults and children for all the sessions. It is hoped that the parent or spiritual guide would act as an encourager for the daily assignments and even do many of them side-by-side with the child, especially the younger child.

In all cases I recommend that a pastor be involved in the process, and, if possible, involve a parent or another adult with the child in the process.

Other suggestions:

—You may want to vary the locations for some of the sessions. If you are meeting one-on-one with the child, you may want to have your meetings in some of the same locations that Pastor Tom and Noah use.

—Begin with a special event. The first session will take more time than the following ones. Why not begin with an overnight retreat or camp setting and work through Chapters 1-3 in a day?

Or begin with an introduction and Chapter 1 following a meal. A pizza supper or lunch is often a good way to start a special relationship with older children. This is a great time to involve parents or other adults.

—Invite a parent, grandparent, or adult friend to write a letter to the child before the first session. Ask him or her to give you the letter to use during the first session. The letter should attempt to affirm the child for his or her gifts, special qualities, and uniqueness. The letter might also express love and affection for the child and a special wish for the child as he or she begins this study.

If the letter is from a parent, there might also be a paragraph about the day when the child was dedicated years ago and the special meaning that the event had for the parents.

Frank Nelson

The Sessions

Materials Needed: student books, Bibles (modern translation such as *Good News Bible*, the Bible in Today's English Version), the mountains of promise already removed from the student book (page 93), scissors, glue or tape, pencils or markers, collection of children's storybooks

Suggested Process

1. Look over some favorite storybooks and ask, "What is one of your all-time favorite stories?"

Thumb through a Bible and ask if there is a favorite Bible story or character they remember.

2. Pass out the student books. Read the section entitled "From the Writer." Ask, "How is a person's life like a story?" (It has a beginning, middle, and end. It involves people, places, events, decisions. It has a plot. There is excitement, tragedy, happiness, and sadness.)

3. Look together at the table of contents and invite the children to insert their own names in the titles for each chapter. Talk about the weeks ahead and give them a little bit of the "flavor" for what will be happening.

Next, invite the children to insert their own names in the title for Chapter 1 and read the introduction under Day One. Invite them to fill in the blanks to their own stories, beginning with "Once upon a time..." and share them with one another.

4. Read the words to the song "I Am a Promise" or listen to the music if you have the record or tape.

Note: The songs in this book are not necessarily intended for singing, but rather, to be read.

Invite the children to write in the box what they think a "Promise and Possibility" means for them. Ask the children to share their ideas. Review some of the thoughts from Baptists around the country.

5. Read the story "A Promise to Noah." There are different approaches for reading a story. Some weeks you may want to read the whole story to the children. Other weeks you may want to take turns allowing the children to read, also.

6. Create the mountain of promise as you discuss the story. (Note: The pattern for the mountain of promise appears in each student's book. It can be pulled out or used as a pattern to make a mountain of promise from construction paper.) Have scissors and clear tape on hand to make these. Also have colored markers for labeling the sides of the mountain. Follow the directions carefully and then label the four sides of the mountain of promise with the words "BODY," "MIND," "SOUL," and "RELATIONSHIPS."

(Important Suggestion: It is probably best to keep the mountains of promise in the leader's possession until the course is completed. They can be easily forgotten or misplaced.)

7. Respond to the story.

—Have you known anyone with cancer? How do you think you would feel if you had cancer? How did Noah describe his feelings in the story?

—Why do you think Noah was interested in getting together with Pastor Tom to talk about a relationship with God and the church?

—Why did Pastor Tom call the paper object a "mountain of promise"? (A mountain is huge, beautiful, and full of potential.)

—Read the story of the promise of God to Noah in Genesis 9:8-17. Try to have the children make a comparison between the Noah of the Bible and the Noah of our story. For example, what was the promise of God to Noah in Genesis, and what do you think was the promise of God to Noah as he faces cancer? (God did not promise that there would be no problems in life, but both Noahs knew that they would always live with God no matter what happened.)

—What do you think God's promise is to you?

8. Introduce the daily activity and emphasize the importance of a daily time of fifteen minutes for Bible study and prayer. Circle the appropriate days as you look over the daily work that is ahead.

9. Establish the time and place for the next meeting.

10. Consider writing a covenant with the children. To do this, simply take a blank sheet of paper and write " I promise that I will..." at the top and leave a place for signatures at the bottom. Decide as the leader what your commitments will be to the children and invite the children to list the things they will be willing to do during the course, such as attending regularly, completing the daily assignments, and praying for one another. Refer back to this on occasion during the course.

11. Invite each person to hold his or her mountain of promise as you lead in a closing prayer such as the following:

Dear God,

Thank you for this new beginning. We're looking forward to spending time together in the weeks ahead. Please guide our study so that all of us will learn more about you and the choices you want us to make for our lives. Thanks for the story of the Bible and for the story of your love for us.

Through Jesus, Amen.

Materials Needed: student books, Bibles, mountains of promise, sodas and/or a snack (optional), paper, pencils and/or markers

Suggested Process

1. Begin with a snack. (You may even want to have this meeting at a favorite inexpensive restaurant. If not, see if you can borrow cups from a McDonald's or similar place for the soda snack.)

Briefly review last week's story and activities. Assume that not all the daily assignments were completed in their entirety. You may want to plan for a significant amount of time for this part of the session. Be sure to affirm the children for the work they have accomplished. Avoid making the person who may not have finished the assignments feel embarrassed or ashamed for not doing it.

Note: The daily assignments are a prelude that helps the children be better prepared for the story and session to come. The material in the daily assignments is an integral part of the whole course and needs to be covered during the session time if it has not been accomplished by the children on their own.

If the class has any new participants, assemble their mountains of promise ahead of time.

2. Turn to Chapter 2 and invite the children to write their names in the chapter title.

Read the story "Golden Arches."

3. Respond to the story.

—When Noah looked up at the golden arches of McDonald's, what do you think he might have been thinking? (rainbow, the promises to Noah, the hope that his treatment would go well)

—What do you think it means to be a "little Christ?"

—Look again at Noah's drawing of God. What does his picture tell you about his view of God in relationship to the world? in relationship to people?

—Discuss Noah's prayer at the end of the story.

> Noah prayed, "Dear God, it's been a good day. I don't know what tomorrow will be like. In fact, I'm scared. But I'm thankful that you have promised me that you will always love me and be with me. I don't want to die, but if I do, I want to be sure that your promise of eternal life is true for me. Please help me to know what it means to give my whole life to you. I really want to be yours. And, God, thanks for Pastor Tom. Amen."

—Read Genesis 1:26-27 and 2:7. Have the children discuss the questions in their student books.

4. Review and discuss the activities for Day Six of last week.

5. Create drawings of God. (Include yourself, too.) Next, invite the children to write a paragraph or a list of words that describe God. (These drawings might be good to display on a bulletin board until the eight weeks of the class are over.)
Share the drawings and descriptions.

6. Review and discuss the activities for day seven of last week.

7. Look ahead at the daily activities for the coming week and circle the appropriate days.

8. Read the words to the song "Breathe on Me, Breath of God," from the student book or from a hymnal.
Reread Noah's prayer at the end of the story (in unison) and close your time in silent prayer.

GUIDE TO CHAPTER 3

Materials Needed: student books, Bibles, bridge-building materials (yarn, tape, twigs or sticks, nonbreakable cups and dishes, bricks, pop cans, play blocks, construction paper, scissors, and so forth)

Suggested Process

1. Build the bridge using the same instructions Pastor Tom used in the story.

2. Turn to Chapter 3 and invite the children to write their names in the chapter title. Next, read the story.

3. Respond to the story. Ask the children such questions as:
—What questions did the story raise for you?
—Noah's stepfather forgave him. What does it mean to forgive someone a wrong that has been done to you? (How is this like God's forgiveness?)
—In what way is Jesus like a bridge to God? (Why do we need a bridge to God?)

4. Review the children's work from the daily activities of the previous week. Be sensitive to any physical or mental disability a child may have. How is sin like breaking a promise?
—Discuss sin as a turning away from God, rather than breaking one or two of the Ten Commandments.

5. Invite the children to look up the Scriptures on the walking bridge illustration and write down a brief description of the importance of each Scripture.

6. Read over some of the "thoughts of Baptists." Discuss them. Share you own story of "coming to Christ" and making the decision to follow him as his disciple.

7. Invite each child to consider praying a prayer of commitment. If this is a group of children, consider some options:
—Lead the group in a guided prayer of commitment. You may want to follow the format that Pastor Tom used in the story.
—Offer to meet individually with each child to talk further and pray together at that time.
—Invite each child to consider praying to God a prayer of commitment in the near future.
—Or wait until the next session when the "decision card" will be introduced.

This is often a sensitive and tender time, but very important. Don't push. If the child is hesitant, acknowledge that and say, "That's OK." Let the decision be the child's, not yours.

8. Invite the children to hold their mountains of promise as you lead in a closing prayer of consecration, such as:

Dear God, You have given us our bodies, minds, relationships, and souls. We offer our whole selves back to you. Forgive us for our sins. Forgive us for breaking our promises to you. Thank you for loving us anyway.
In Jesus' name, amen.

GUIDE TO CHAPTER 4

Materials Needed: student books, Bibles, pencils, mountains of promise, decision cards copied from those in the book (optional)

My Decisions

I believe that God has invited me to follow Jesus as my Lord and Savior, my bridge to God, and to give my whole life—mind, body, relationships, and soul—to God. Therefore, these are my decisions...

yes **not yet**

____ ____ 1. I believe Jesus Christ is God's Son and accept him as my Lord and Savior.

____ ____ 2. I will try to live as a true follower of Jesus Christ at all times and in all places.

____ ____ 3. I will think and pray about what it means to be a follower of Jesus Christ before making a decision to be baptized and become a member of my church.

____ ____ 4. I wish to be baptized.

____ ____ 5. I wish to become a member of my church.

____ ____ 6. Other decisions:

____

____

____

____

____

Signature ______________________________

Date ______________________________

Suggested Process

1. Invite the children to write their names in the title to this week's chapter.

2. Read the words to the song. Using paints and brushes, demonstrate the mixing of blue and yellow paints to make green. Discuss the meaning of the song in light of this illustration.

3. Review the daily work for days three and four of last week. Discuss the meaning of the words "Lord" and "Savior."

4. Read the story "On Golden Wings."

—How did Pastor Tom describe the church in the story? How would you describe "the church"?

—Study the poster on the inside cover of an extra student's book. Ask the children questions such as this: What are some symbols of the Christian life that you see in this picture?

—At the end of the story Noah felt that he belonged. To whom? Why?

—Do you think it was a good idea for Noah to postpone his decision to be baptized until he could learn more about it? What are some reasons that might have made him hesitate to be baptized?

5. Review the daily work for days five, six, and seven.

As you discuss church membership, include some of the following ideas. Decide whether or not the child is mature enough to respond to the abstract ideas.

We join the church:

a. for companionship and encouragement in living as disciples of Christ. Church members and worship help feed the "soul" part of our mountains of promise.

b. because our church is our spiritual family. It is an important part of the "relationships" section of our mountains of promise.

c. to support the things that churches do–mission work, teaching about Jesus, working for justice and peace.

d. because the church is the body of Christ. By joining the church it is a symbol and public expression that we are in partnership with the people who carry out Jesus' ministry.

You might introduce these ideas by asking, "Why do people join the church?"

6. Have the children fill in the "Worksheet About My Church." If this was done at home, there may be some information still needed. Expand this information as much as you would like. Supplement this material with brochures or pamphlets about your church that will be descriptive.

7. Preview the daily assignments for the coming week and circle the appropriate days.

8. Encourage each child to fill out his or her decision card (either in the book or a separate card copied from the book) sometime during the coming week. At this time it is appropriate to fill out only numbers 1, 2, and 3. (Some children may want to wait until after the discussion on baptism and church membership before making decisions on numbers 4 and 5.)

Hold the decision cards in hand as you lead a closing prayer about the decisions that each child will make.

GUIDE TO CHAPTER 5

Materials Needed: student books, Bibles, pencils, building block materials (wood blocks and/or other materials for building, with four blocks labeled "worship," "mission," "community," and "education")

Suggested Process

1. Invite the children to write their names in the title of this week's chapter. Read in unison "We Are Gifts of God" from Day Two of last week's daily work. Discuss any parts of this that seem appropriate.

2. Read the story "Building-Block Church."

3. Respond to the story.
   —What were the four building blocks of the church that Rev. Nan described? Give your own definition of each.
   —Rev. Nan sang the first line to "The Church's One Foundation Is Jesus Christ Her Lord." What do you think it means to say that Jesus is the foundation of the church? (You may want to look this one up in your church hymnal and look at some more of the words.)
   —At the end of the story Noah corrected Rev. Nan by saying, "You mean the church *building*." What is the difference between the "church" and the "church building"? Review and discuss the words to the song at the beginning of the chapter, "We Are the Church."
   —Noah said, "Count me in." What did he mean by that?

4. Create your own building-block church. Discuss the four blocks that represent worship, education, community or fellowship, and mission. Talk about ways children can be involved in each one of them.

5. Review the daily work from last week (days 4, 5, 6, and 7) to think about the promises we make to the church.

6. Invite the children to share any decisions they may have made on their decision cards.

7. Preview the daily work for the coming week and circle the appropriate days. Invite them to be considering their decision for numbers 4 and 5 on the decision card.

8. Close with prayer.

GUIDE TO CHAPTER 6

Materials Needed: student books, Bibles, mountains of promise, grape juice, bread

Suggested Process

(If this study has been undertaken by a parent or other adult with their child, it is recommended that this session be led by the pastor.)

1. Gather around the Communion table of your church. (You may decide to invite someone who helps to prepare the elements for Communion to join you for this session.) Introduce today's class. As you do, invite the children to consider today as another day of deciding. If they have not already done so, they will be invited to make a decision about numbers 4 and 5 on the decision card at the end of today's session.

2. Read the words to the song "I Have Decided to Follow Jesus" at the beginning of Chapter 6. Also invite the children to write their names in the chapter title for this session.

3. Read the story "Bread and Water."

4. Discuss the story.

—What do you think were some of the reasons that held Noah back from wanting to be baptized?

—Do you have any fears, questions, or uncertainties about baptism?

—After reading the story, do you see any connections or similarities between Communion and baptism? What are they? (the themes of death and covenant)

—At the end, Noah says to Alex, "I'll tell you all about it." Finish the story. You may even want to role-play or act it out. What do you think Noah told Alex? What might have been his friend's reaction?

5. Review the daily work from last week and discuss some of the information from days four through seven. As you do, allow the children to enter the baptism tank (if that's possible). Explain in detail what happens during a baptism. Demonstrate how a person is laid in the water and talk about the symbols involved in baptism. Attempt to relieve the fears that they may have about baptism.

During your discussion of Communion, gather around the table and talk in detail about the meaning of the bread and cup. If you have invited a person who helps to prepare Communion, ask him or her to enter the discussion and share with the children what he or she believes the symbols mean and why Communion is important. It may be appropriate if the children have made a decision to follow Jesus on their decision cards to offer the bread and cup to them. This may be the first time some children have ever taken Communion, depending on the custom of our individual churches. Other churches may require that baptism precede Communion.

6. Repeat the words to the song "I Have Decided to Follow Jesus." Then return to the decision card to allow each child to mark his or her decision about baptism and church membership. If the children would like to continue to think about this decision, encourage them to take the card home with them and return it whenever they are ready. (Follow up, however, with a visit or phone call.)

7. Preview the next session and circle the appropriate days for the daily work.

8. Close with a prayer of commitment and thanksgiving.

GUIDE TO CHAPTER 7

Materials Needed: student books, Bibles, posters or pictures of a bridge, mountains of promise

Suggested Process

1. Begin this session by pointing out to the children that the inside covers of their books will become a bridge poster. Review how Jesus is our bridge to God. Ask the children to begin thinking of ways in which we can be like bridges, too.
   Invite the children to write their names in the chapter title.

2. Read the story "The Golden Gate."

3. Discuss the story. Use these questions that are also in the children's book.
   —At the end of the story Noah feels that he is like a bridge. What does that mean to you?
   —How is "Meals On Wheels" like a bridge for God?
   —What do you think Pastor Tom means when he says, "But I tell you, there's so much that needs to be done for God in this world that it's going to take a lot of Golden Gate Bridges like you and me to accomplish it?"

4. Reread Luke 4:18-19 and discuss each part of the verse in relationship to what you might be able to do as a bridge for God.

5. Review the daily work from last week and talk about how each prophet and each Baptist from history was like a bridge.

6. Name people you know from your church and ways in which they are serving God and others by being a bridge outside your church.

Name	**How are they serving?**

7. Offer several suggestions to the children of ways they can be involved in the mission of your congregation. Invite them to commit themselves to involvement in at least one thing.

8. Make any final plans in preparation for the baptism.

9. Preview the daily work for the coming week and circle the appropriate days.

Arrange for the time of last session. (The final session may be best after the date of the baptism as a celebration of the baptism as well as a new motivation for living the Christian life.)

10. Close your time together by reading or singing the song at the beginning of the chapter, "They'll Know We Are Christians by Our Love."

Lead in a closing prayer.

GUIDE TO CHAPTER 8

Materials Needed: student books, Bibles, children's devotional books and magazines, mountains of promise, Bible study tools

Suggested Process

1. Invite the children to put their names in the title at the beginning of the chapter.

2. For this session you may want to return to McDonald's or another favorite spot. Bring along some bottles of vitamins or pictures of food that represent a well-balanced diet. Discuss with the children the importance of good nutrition.

3. Read the story "Good Nutrition."

4. Discuss the story. Use some of the questions and guidelines in the student book.
   —"He was the same old Noah, but he felt like gold." How do you interpret the meaning of that line in the story? Do you think that Noah was a different person in some ways?
   —Why do you suppose Noah wanted to tell everyone about it?
   —Why do you suppose that Noah enjoyed reading the Bible more now?
   —List some of the disciplines mentioned in the story for good nutrition (health) in the Christian life.

   ____

   ____

   ____

   ____

   ____

   ____

   ____

5. Review the daily work from Chapter 7 in the book. Discuss in detail the importance of prayer, Bible study, stewardship, and witness. Show the children a concordance, Bible dictionary, and atlas. Offer some suggestions for children's devotional books and magazines.

6. Create a plan for growth. Help the children be specific about their own plans for growth. Try to be as helpful as possible with each as they create their plan. Also share your own growth plan for spiritual health and some of the things that you have found most helpful in your Christian life.

   Use this space so that you will have something of your own to share that will be brief and to the point.

My Plan for Personal Christian Growth

My plan for personal daily prayer. ______________________

____

____

My plan for personal Bible study and devotion. ___________

____

____

My plan for giving. ________________________________

____

____

My plan for witness. _______________________________

____

____

My plan for involvement in my church. _______________

____

____

My plan for mission and service. ____________________

____

____

____

(signature) date

7. Share the plans with one another. After each one shares, the group can respond with: "__________________(the name of the person), you are a mountain of promise!"

8. Review some of the thoughts on church membership from Baptists around the country.

9. Invite children to participate in a closing prayer by completing each phrase in the following prayer:

   Dear God,

   I praise you...

   I'm sorry I...

   Thank you for...

   Help me...

   In Jesus' name, amen.

Express some closing words of thanks and love and invite the children to join with you in reading in unison the words to the song at the beginning of Chapter 8, "Love, Do This and Live," by Rich Roberts.

Resources for Children's Leaders

About Faith and Your Child

A Scriptographic Booklet by Channing L. Bete Co., Inc. A firm foundation in Christ gives children strength to meet the challenges of growth.

Children as Partners in the Church

D-B and Phyllis Heusser. "Let's grow together" is the theme of this refreshing "partnership" concept in which children and adults learn together, worship as a church family, participate in mission, and grow in faith. Innovative partnership ideas are designed to give children a sense of belonging by involving them in every aspect of church life.

Helping Your Child Discover Faith

Delia Touchton Halverson. Shows parents simple ways for sharing God's love in the everyday happenings of a child's world. Together parent and child learn to enjoy God as a personal friend.

Books on this list are available through Judson Mail Order, 1-800-4-JUDSON or P.O. Box 851, Valley Forge, PA 19482-0851, or at your local Christian bookstore.

Faith Development of Older Elementary Children

by Eula Fresch

When you begin using this discipleship course with children, questions will arise about their faith development. What has led up to the decision to involve them in a series of sessions related to the meaning of discipleship and church membership? In what ways do they seem ready to take on the responsibilities and privileges of membership in your congregation? What or who has prepared (is preparing) them to make a decision for Christ and his church? What is the church doing to encourage children in their lifelong growth as disciples, that is, in their faith development?

When we think about the faith development of children in grades five and six, we must first determine what we mean by faith and what the dimensions of the Christian faith are. We must then think about what we mean by *faith development*. We must also see the faith development of older elementary children in relation to the total life journey of faith. It is important to be aware of how they have developed from early childhood to the present and consider in what direction they may be moving as they become youth and adults. We need to know what we can expect of them at this age. Once we have this background, we can consider ways we can help these boys and girls grow in faith. For example, what specific things can the family and church do? Finally, we must examine where we are in our own faith journey, how we got to this point, and how we can personally share our own living, growing faith with these children.

What thoughts come to your mind when you think about the word "faith"? Different meanings have been given to this word. It is spoken of in the psychological sense of building trust and in the religious sense of belief in and commitment to God. John Hendrick in *Opening the Door of Faith* says that faith has to do with deep convictions and core values arising from encountering and experiencing the gospel, life, and God. He contrasts faith with belief and religion. Belief has to do with what we think about our faith convictions, theological interpretations, statements of purpose and goals, creeds and so on. Hendrick says religion refers to what we do and ways we behave in the church and in the world.[1] Thomas Groome in *Christian Religious Education* speaks of faith as having three dimensions expressed in three activities: (1) believing, (2) trusting, and (3) doing. Groome emphasizes that faith is always the gift of God. He explains that although we cannot give "faith" to anyone, the Christian community must share its faith and support people in their faith journeys.[2]

Faith development is a lifelong process. Our development in faith goes through stages, according to John Westerhoff and James Fowler. Westerhoff and Fowler each have theories about faith development. Westerhoff compares faith development to tree development in this way:

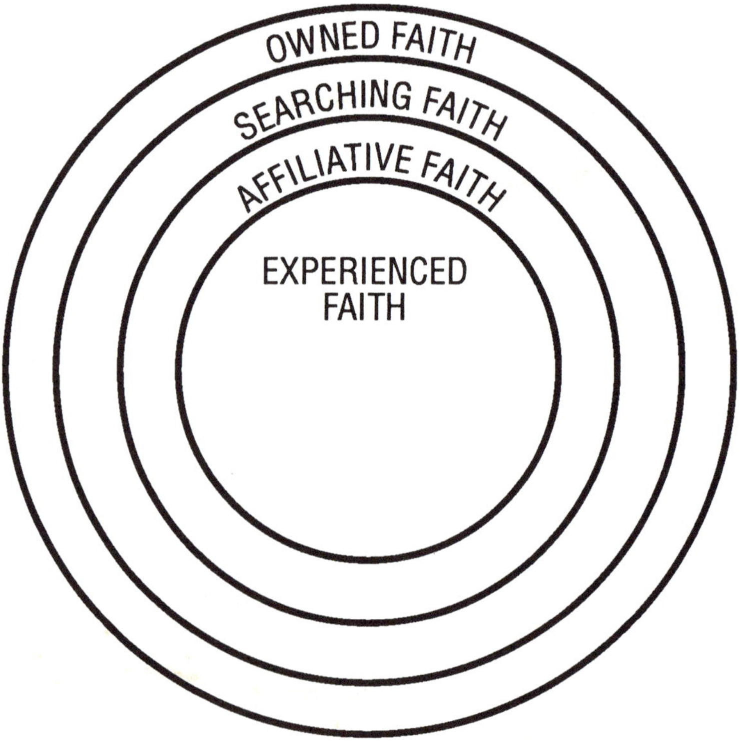

[1] John R. Hendrick, *Opening the Door of Faith: How Evangelism Works*. Atlanta: John Knox Press, 1977.
[2] Thomas Groome, *Christian Religious Education*. New York: Harper & Row, Publishers, Inc. 1982.

The faith development theories of Westerhoff and Fowler are summarized in the following excerpt from "Personal Becoming and Life Stages," by Richard Olson, printed in the September 1984 issues of *Baptist Leader* (vol. 46, no. 6) pp. 4-5.

Styles of Faith

John Westerhoff speaks of styles of faith. He points out that he conceives of faith as a verb, a way of behaving that involves knowing, being, and willing. He sees faith as an action. In noting four styles of faith, he points out that each is complete in itself, as a tree of any age is complete in itself. In each stage (or style) the previous remains, as the rings of growth remain when one cuts across a tree that has existed for years. His styles or stages, then, are:

1. *Experienced faith*. During preschool and early childhood years the child explores and reacts with others who offer the child the basic experiences that constitute faith at that time. As children are hugged, caressed, stroked, and treated faithfully, they respond with faith appropriate to that time of their lives.

2. *Affiliative faith*. This stage comes in childhood and early adolescent years when one seeks to act with others in a community. The marks of this stage are a sense of *belonging*, the dominance of religious *affections*, and a sense of *authority* of the community's story.

3. *Searching faith*. In late adolescence and young adult years a searching faith may expand into a mode of faithing, where some of the characteristics are *doubt* or *critical judgment*; the need to *experiment* and *explore* other life-styles and faith stances than those of one's heritage; and the awareness of the need to *commit*.

4. *Owned style of faith*. If the needs of searching faith have been met, one may move into an *owned style of faith*. Such persons still have questions but are willing to stand on what they believe. They want to put their faith into personal and social action.

Westerhoff points out that though persons often see the movement from *searching* to *owned faith* as "conversion," really the whole process of faith development is conversion.[1]

[1] John J. Westerhoff III, *Will Our Children Have Faith?* (New York: Seabury Press, 1976), pp. 89-99.

Faith-Development Stages

James W. Fowler and associates have carried on an extensive research through interviews and reflection. Out of this they have constructed a rather elaborate theory of faith development through six stages.

Stage 1: *Intuitive-Projective Faith*. For children of ages four to eight, this is a time when life is fantasy-filled, when the child constantly encounters new objects and experiences. The child is imitative of important adults and is influenced by their examples, moods, actions, and stories. There is fluidity of thought and active imagination to make sense of one's world.

Stage 2. *Mythic-Literal Faith*. The typical age range is from six to twelve. The child takes on for himself or herself the stories, beliefs, and observances that belong to one's community. Beliefs, moral rules, and attitudes are interpreted literally. Symbols also are seen as one-dimensional and literal in meaning.

Stage 3: *Synthetic-Conventional Faith*. This stage may begin as early as age eleven or twelve. Some persons begin to move out of it in their late teens, but for many it starts later and continues on throughout the rest of their lives. In this stage much more complex values and information must be synthesized. The person structures the ultimate environment in interpersonal terms. For the most part it is a conformist stage. The person is carefully tuned to the expectations and judgments of important others. One does not yet have a sure enough grasp on one's own identity to feel free to construct one's own unique perspective.

Stage 4: *Individuating-Reflexive Faith*. The transition into this stage may occur in the late teens, more frequently in the twenties, and for some much later—in the thirties or forties. Now one takes seriously the burden of responsibility for one's own commitments, beliefs, attitudes, and life-style. One experiences tensions in doing so, such as tension between individuality and group identity. Symbols and stories may diminish in significance, while critical reflection and the ability to form the judgement ("Here I stand; I can do no other") are in the forefront of one's faithing.

Stage 5: *Conjunctive Faith*. Fowler notes that rarely does a person enter Stage 5 before age thirty, although some persons who have suffered disadvantage, discrimination, or oppression may confront Stage-5 issues and adopt Stage-5 perspectives earlier than others. For the most part, it is rare before mid-life, and many never come to it at all. At this stage, one integrates into one's self and outlook much that was suppressed in the critical searching of Stage 4. One's symbols, stories, and myths in one's heritage are reclaimed in a reworking of one's past. One has absorbed "the sacrament of defeat" and understands the reality of irrevocable commitments and acts. One understands and enters into paradox; one is able to unify opposites in mind and experience. Through deep convictions, one is able to be vulnerable and open to the strange truths of those who are other. Conviction, tolerance, and peace with what one claims as one's own out of one's faith heritage are all woven together in this stage of faith.

Stage 6: Universalizing Faith. Even more rare than Stage 5, universalizing faith is experienced by a few rare individuals. The person in this stage senses a call to be incarnator and actualizer of the ideal that includes an inclusive and fulfilled human community. Says Fowler of them, "Many persons in this stage die at the hands of those whom they hope to change. Universalizers are often more honored and revered after death than during their lives."[2] Inclusiveness of all in their vision of community, radical commitment to justice and love, selfless passion for a transformed world—these are the marks of a Stage-6 person.

Fowler points out that each stage has the "potential for wholeness, grace, and integrity and for strengths sufficient for either life's blows or blessings."[3] One should not look at this list and be anxious to hurry on to the next stage. However, one should be open to growth and progression, for each new stage marks the rise of new strengths and capacities in faith which add to and interact with all the previous strengths one might have possessed.[4]

[2] James W. Fowler, *Stages of Faith* (San Francisco: Harper & Row, Publishers, Inc., 1981), p. 201.
[3] James W. Fowler, *Stages of Faith* (San Francisco: Harper & Row, Publishers, Inc., 1981), p. 274.
[4] *Ibid.*, p. 274. This description was taken from *Stages of Faith*, pp. 118-211, and from Jim Fowler and Sam Keen, *Life Maps: Conversations on the Journey of Faith* (Minneapolis: Winston Press, Inc., 1978), pp. 14-99.

Faith and the Community of Faith

The following illustrations and descriptions help to further explain these stages in relation to community.

Stage 0
0-4 years
The Child relates to
one or two significant adults.

Stage 1
4-7 or 8 years
The Child still needs relationships with significant adults but also has *child-child relationships*. These are usually of a parallel nature.

Stage 2
7-11 or 12 years
The Child's *peer group* (the gang) is the most significant relationship.

Stage 3
12-17 or 18 years
Belonging is the key to relationships at this stage. The child, youth or adult's family, ethnic group, particular church or play or work group is central to growth in faith. Emotions are important in worship.

Stage 4

Accepting responsibility and making judgments may cause *tensions between individuality and group identity*. Ideas are important in worship.

Stage 5

Adults at this stage often *relate to a number of groups* and can move in and out of them and *take stands unacceptable to any of the groups*. Ideas and emotions are important in worship.

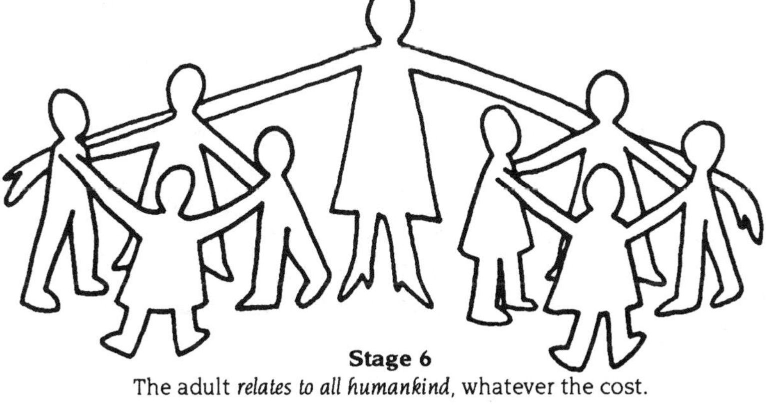

Stage 6

The adult *relates to all humankind*, whatever the cost.

The work of Westerhoff and Fowler help us understand much about faith development. However, it is important to remember that each person is unique and the stages described are ones that people may or may not pass through. The ages are suggestions and not meant to be used to label or to limit. Groome points out "the mystery of human life and becoming can never be captured totally in any easy outline of stages" (Groome, p. 66).

Ways to Foster Faith Development

With this background information in mind we can now focus on specific ways of helping children in their faith journeys. One way is to make sure parents are aware of the role they play in their children's faith development. Experiencing love, trust, and acceptance in the home, going to church with parents, praying with them, and seeing the examples parents set as they grow in the faith are some of the ways faith development can be fostered in the home.

Stephen Jones, in his book *Faith Shaping*, has the following ideas for teachers and leaders who are open to the Holy Spirit at work in and through them.

*Nurturing Children for Commitment**

As teachers who are open to the Holy Spirit at work in and through us, we will nurture each child by:

1. *Telling Bible Stories.* We will help each child become very familiar and comfortable with the Bible. We will do this by sharing those parts a child can easily understand: stories and incidents rather than highly symbolic passages (for example, emphasize Paul's travels, actions, and personality rather than his theological formulations). Our hope will be that each child will come to love the Bible as a book of exciting incidents, real people, and an exciting and real God. It will not seem distant, hard to read, or complicated. As teachers we will appreciate each child's interpretations and nurture him or her in ways that will help each one grow in understanding of the Scripture.

*Adapted from *Faith Shaping* by Stephen D. Jones (Valley Forge: Judson Press, 1980), p. 73.

2. *Modeling Our Adult Faith*. Children will observe our adult faith in worship, in congregational life, in mission and will use it as a model for their own faith development.

3. *Helping Them Develop Key Christian Concepts*. These are a basic part of the foundation for children's more mature faith as adults. They need help in refining such concepts as life, love, sharing, caring, death, right and wrong, hope, honesty, joy, peace, anger, pride, power, wonder, justice, God, the Bible, church, and promise. With the help of curriculum resources and church membership materials we will enable children to explore a concept by (a) reading about it, (b) acting it out, (c) playing games based upon it, (d) "crafting" things from it, (e) relating it to life, (f) testing it upon life, and (g) reflecting on their experiences.

4. *Encouraging Their Natural Ability to Wonder, to Question, to Create, to Imagine, and to Initiate*. By doing so each child will develop specific skills to use in one's faith-shaping tasks as adolescence approaches.

5. *Helping Them to Interpret Life's Experiences in Light of the Gospel*. Children are very curious. We will encourage their asking "Why," "How," and "When," knowing that practice at interpretation of life's experiences is the beginning of a faith-shaping skill.

6. *Helping Them Build a Rich Repertoire of Memories*. Persons who have no important memories of the faith, of the church, of an experience of God, or of spiritual feelings will find themselves in a faith vacuum as youth and young adults.

7. *Affirming Children*. We will work to provide a church family of faith that is a warm, inviting, and welcoming one that accepts children where they are. We will help them build self-esteem based on being created in the image of God.

It is important to be aware of the vital role the entire atmosphere of church life plays in the children's faith development. Are opportunities provided for the children to make a contribution, give leadership, and participate in the ministry of the church at their level? Are they included in activities where they have the opportunity to relate with church members of all ages? Are opportunities provided for members to share their faith with the children? Do they feel loved and accepted within the church family?

Think about each boy and girl in your group. What has influenced each one's development up to this point? What has been the influence of the home, the extended family, the school, and the church? How involved is each family and child in the life of the church? What experiences are lacking? What experiences does each child need now? How will this study, *Bridges of Promise*, help him or her grow? In answering these questions it is important to keep in mind that faith development is interrelated with all areas of the child's development.

Finally, examine your own journey of faith. List the people and experiences that have helped your discipleship. Where are you in your faith journey now? What are the times and places in which you and other church members can share your faith with each child? Remember, faith is relational, so this sharing and interacting is vital. As you and others in the church share your faith journeys, the Holy Spirit works through you and the children to enhance their growth as disciples.

The following resources may be helpful:

Cully, Iris V., *Christian Child Development*. San Francisco: Harper & Row, Publisher, Inc., 1979.

Halverson, Delia, *Helping Your Child Discover Faith*. Valley Forge: Judson Press, 1982.

Westerhoff, John H., *Bringing Up Children in the Christian Faith*. Minneapolis: Winston Press, 1980.

Eula Fresch, Ed.D., has been an editor of children's levels of Judson Bible Series. She has been a faculty member of Eastern Baptist Theological Seminary, Philadelphia, PA. As a parent, she has personal experience in nurturing her child in the faith.

Editor's note: Here is one pastor's way of responding to requests of young children for baptism. Excerpted from an article in *Baptist Leader,** it is offered here to stimulate dialogue on how to encourage children in their search for belonging in the community of faith.

Children and Church Membership

by Douglas Hargis

A thought-provoking editorial by a regional executive minister caught my attention one day. It noted that while we as Baptists do not believe in infant baptism, our practice often included the baptism of children at an age when they were really too young to understand what they were doing.

This came home to me when a member of our congregation came to me at about age twenty-five and asked to be rebaptized. She explained that she had been baptized when she was about eleven, but did not really understand what being a Christian was all about. In her mind her newly awakened understanding seemed to warrant a re-baptism.

Then one day the inevitable happened—two young boys approached me following a service of baptism with the request that they be baptized. These boys were eight years old, children of faithful members of the church. Both boys had grown up in our Sunday school, so I was not too surprised when they approached me. I shared my joy over their decision and made appointments to talk with each one.

The challenge of that executive minister and the experience of that young woman kept eating away at my conscience. As I listened to the experience of each of these two boys, I decided to have both boys in a four-week "baptism class." It became increasingly clear to me that they were not yet ready for baptism. It also became increasingly clear to me that these two boys had a very sincere, genuine love for Jesus. I was on the horns of a dilemma.

*Spring 1991

The Dilemma

Was I to go ahead and baptize these boys, even though they could not adequately understand the faith, or was I to say no and run the risk of them feeling rejected by the minister and, in their young hearts, by God? The essence of my struggle became this: How can I affirm their eight-year-old love for Jesus without performing a baptism that would not be very meaningful? There was nothing in my Baptist tradition to answer that question, so I began to reflect on the life of Jesus.

Jesus was baptized when he was about thirty years of age. He certainly understood what he was doing. As an infant, Jesus was dedicated by his parents in the temple. At age twelve, he experienced his bar mitzvah in the Jewish faith. We do not have a record of any other ceremony taking place earlier in his life.

As Jesus went about his public ministry, he encouraged baptism. How old were those baptized? The texts do not say specifically, but we do know that these persons were old enough to understand what sin was, confess it, and repent of it. It seems that these were adults, not children. Children had a different experience with Jesus. Out of that experience I found a solution to the dilemma.

During the parental dedication of children, we make reference to the event of Jesus' life where parents were bringing their children to Jesus to bless them. This is usually interpreted to be infants being brought to Jesus. Indeed, if we examine the passage from Luke's Gospel (Luke 18:15-17), we see that Luke used the specific word "infants" ("babies," NIV) at verse 15 to describe the ones being brought to Jesus to be touched (with a blessing implied). Jesus then responded with the more general term "children" (verses 16 and 17), by inviting the *children* to himself, in spite of the disapproval of the disciples. This more general term included not only infants but all children through age twelve, prior to the age of bar mitzvah. While some parents were bringing infants, Jesus invited children of all ages to receive a blessing, not a baptism.

A look at the parallel passages in Mark (10:13-16) and Matthew (19:13-15) reveals that only the general term "children" is used. The children receiving a blessing were not simply infants, but children of all ages prior to bar mitzvah. Jesus knew that children were capable of responding to him in genuine love, but that they were not yet ready for baptism, which required a more mature understanding of sin and repentance. He affirmed that the kingdom of God belongs to ones with a childlike faith and affirmed that faith with a blessing, not a baptism.

An Answer

Here was the answer to my dilemma. I would create a service patterned after this example from the life of our Lord and call it a "Service of the Lord's Blessing." While affirming the sincere love for Jesus that young children can develop, it would reserve baptism for a time in life when they are capable of a more mature understanding of sin, repentance, and the Lordship of Christ.

Having decided in my mind what to do, the next question to be answered was, Would it work? Would this service satisfy the spiritual hunger in the lives of these boys, or would they still feel rejected? All I could do was give it a try.

It worked! The boys responded positively, and now I have no hesitation about suggesting to young children (ages six to nine) that we affirm their sincere love for Jesus with a "Service of the Lord's Blessing" and reserve the experience of baptism for later, when they can have a better understanding of their Christian faith.

The service itself is fairly simple. The ceremony is part of the regular Sunday morning worship. It is for the individual child—no other children or parents are involved in the ceremony. I call the child forward at the appropriate time. I read Mark 10:13-16 and also Matthew 18:1-6, 10. Then I explain some of the background leading to the presence of the child before them—the child's dedication as an infant, nurture in the faith at home and in the Sunday school, and the child's response of love for Jesus. Then I use the example from the life of Jesus regarding the blessing of children, older ones as well as infants, to explain the significance of this ceremony.

Following this introduction I pick up the child and hold him or her (if that is physically possible—if not, then I place my hands upon the child). I then comment to the congregation about the child's love for Jesus and about young faith. Then I recite a verse of Scripture which may be chosen especially to suit the character of the child or may be simply John 3:16 with the child's name inserted at the appropriate places in the verse. Finally, with hands still on the child, I pronounce a blessing upon the child, affirming God's love for her or him. The child then returns to his or her seat.

This service is by no means a standard procedure that everyone in the Sunday school will experience when one reaches a certain age. Rather it is reserved for those youngsters who take some initiative regarding baptism or church membership.

Jesus said, "Let the little children come to me; do not stop them; for it is to such as these that the Kingdom of God belongs" (Mark 10:14, NRSV). What are the implications of that statement for Baptists regarding the baptism of children? What would Jesus say?

Douglas Hargis is the pastor of the First Baptist Church in Kenton, Ohio.

The Judson Church Membership/Discipleship Resources were prepared in part through the use of funds provided by the George Dana and Ella C. Boardman Grant of Educational Ministries, ABC/USA. George Dana Boardman authored a booklet, *The Problem of Jesus*, which is available upon request from:

Judson Press
P.O. Box 851
Valley Forge, PA 19482-0851